GIMP 2.8 Shortcuts

By

U. C-Abel Books.

All Rights Reserved

First Edition: 2017

Copyright @ U. C-Abel Books. **ISBN-13: 978-1979461191**

ISBN-13: 978-1979461191
ISBN-10: 1979461198

Published by U. C-Abel Books.

Table of Contents

Acknowledgement.

We thank God for the completion of this book.

We sincerely appreciate GNU (GNU's Not Unix) for their hard work and ceaseless efforts in making sure the public is provided with helpful programs and resources that are totally free.

We also thank our lovely readers who are never tired of reading our publications.

We wish you well.

Dedication

This title is dedicated to GIMP 2.8 users all over the world.

Introduction

After thinking of how to help computer users become more productive in their operation of computers and various fields, it came to our knowledge that there is a smart option many computer users ignore easily and that part has a high yielding capacity that is known to just few people.

We went into deep research to broaden our knowledge of key combination and found it very helpful. So we started this series "Shortcut Matters" including tips, techniques, keyboard shortcuts, and packaging the title in a way it will attract readers and get a high rating class just to help you.

Relax and make your mind ready for learning as we go.

What to Know Before You Begin.

General Notes.

1. Most of the keyboard shortcuts you will see in this book refer to the U.S. keyboard layout. Keys for other layouts might not correspond exactly to the keys on a U.S. keyboard. Keyboard shortcuts for laptop computers might also differ.

2. It is important to note that when using shortcuts to perform any command, you should make sure the target area is active, if not, you may get a wrong result. Example, if you want to highlight all texts you must make sure the text field is active and if an object, make sure the object area is active. The active area is always known by the location where the cursor of your computer blinks.

3. The plus (+) sign that comes in the middle of keyboard shortcuts simply means the keys are meant to be combined or held down together not to be added as one of the shortcut keys. In a case where plus sign is needed; it will be duplicated (++).

4. Many keyboards assign special functions to function keys, by default. To use the function key for other purposes, you have to press Fn+the function key.

5. It is also important to note that the keyboard shortcuts listed in this book are to be used in GIMP 2.8.

6. To get more information on this title visit ucabelbooks.wordpress.com and search the site using keywords related to it.

7. Our chief website is under construction.

Some Short Forms You Will Find in This Book and Their Full Meaning.

Here are short forms used in this GIMP 2.8 Shortcuts book and their full meaning.

1.	Tab	-	Tabulate Key
2.	Shft	-	Shift Key
3.	F	-	Function Key
4.	Esc	-	Escape Key
5.	Ctrl	-	Control Key
6.	Alt	-	Alternate Key

CHAPTER 1.

15 (Fifteen) Special Keyboard Shortcuts.

The fifteen special keyboard shortcuts are fifteen (15) shortcuts every computer user should know.

The following is a list of keyboard shortcuts every computer user should know:

1. **Ctrl + A:** Control A, highlights or selects everything you have in the environment where you are working.

   *If you are like **"Wow, the content of this document is large and there is no time to select all of it, besides, it's going to mount pressure on my computer?"** Using the mouse for this is an outdated method of handling a task like selecting all, Ctrl+A will take care of that in a second.*

2. **Ctrl + C:** Control C copies any highlighted or selected element within the work environment.

   Saves the time and stress which would have been used to right click and click again just to copy. Use ctrl+c.

3. **Ctrl + N:** Control N opens a new window or file.

   Instead of clicking **File**, **New**, **blank/ template** *and another* **click**, *just press* **Ctrl + N** *and a fresh page or window will appear instantly.*

4. **Ctrl + O:** Control O opens a new program.

   Use ctrl +O when you want to locate / open a file or program.

5. **Ctrl + P:** Control P prints the active document.

   Always use this to locate the printer dialog box, and thereafter print.

6. **Ctrl + S:** Control S saves a new document or file and changes made by the user.

   Please stop! Don't use the mouse. Just press Ctrl+S and everything will be saved.

7. **Ctrl +V:** Control V pastes copied elements into the active area of the program in use.

Using ctrl+V in a case like this Saves the time and stress of right clicking and clicking again just to paste.

8. **Ctrl + W:** Control W is used to close the page you are working on when you want to leave the work environment.

>   ***"There is a way Debby does this without using the mouse. Oh my God, why didn't I learn it then?"*** Don't worry, I have the answer. Debby presses Ctrl+W to close active windows.

9. **Ctrl + X:** Control X cuts elements (making the elements to disappear from their original place). The difference between cutting and deleting elements is that in Cutting, what was cut doesn't get lost permanently but prepares itself so that it can be pasted on another location defined by the user.

>   *Use ctrl+x when you think **"this shouldn't be here and I can't stand the stress of retyping or redesigning it on the rightful place it belongs".***

10. **Ctrl + Y:** Control Y redoes actions.

Ctrl+Z brought back what you didn't need? Press Ctrl+ Y to remove it again.

11. **Ctrl + Z:** Control Z undoes actions.
Can't find what you typed now or a picture you inserted, it suddenly disappeared or you mistakenly removed it? Press Ctrl+Z to bring it back.

12. **Alt + F4:** Alternative F4 closes active windows or items.

*You don't need to move the mouse in order to close an active window, just press **Alt + F4**. Also use it when you are done or you don't want somebody who is coming to see what you are doing.*

13. **Ctrl + F6:** Control F6 Navigates between open windows, making it possible for a user to see what is happening in windows that are active.
Are you working in Microsoft Word and want to find out if the other active window where your browser is loading a page is still progressing? Use Ctrl + F6.

14. **F1:** This displays the help window.

*Is your computer malfunctioning? Use **F1** to find help when you don't know what next to do.*

15. **F12:** This enables users to make changes to an already saved document.

> *F12 is the shortcut to use when you want to change the format in which you saved your existing document, password it, change its name, change the file location or destination, or make other changes to it. It will save you time.*

Note: The Control (Ctrl) key on Windows and Linux operating system is the same thing as Command (Cmmd) key on a Macintosh computer. So if you replace Control with Command key on a Mac computer for the special shortcuts listed above, you will get the same result.

CHAPTER 2.

Fundamental Knowledge of Keyboard Shortcuts.

Without the existence of the keyboard, there wouldn't have been anything like keyboard shortcuts so in this chapter we will learn a little about the computer keyboard before moving to keyboard shortcuts.

1. Definition of Computer Keyboard.

This is an input device that is used to send data to computer memory.

1.1 Types of Keyboard.

   i. Standard (Basic) Keyboard.

   ii. Enhanced (Extended) Keyboard.

   i. **Standard Keyboard:** This a keyboard designed during the 1800s for mechanical typewriters with just 10 function keys (F keys) placed at the left side of it.

ii. **Enhanced Keyboard:** This is the current 101 to 102-key keyboard that is included in almost all the personal computers (PCs) of nowadays, which has 12 function keys, usually at the top side of it.

1.2 Segments of the keyboard

- Numeric keys.
- Alphabetic keys.
- Punctuation keys.
- Windows Logo key.
- Function keys.
- Special keys.

Numeric Keys: Numeric keys are keys with numbers from **0 - 9**.

Alphabetic Keys: These are keys that have alphabets on them, ranging from **A** to **Z**.

Punctuation Keys: These are keys of the keyboard used for punctuation, examples include comma, full stop, colon, question marks, hyphen, etc.

Windows Logo Key: A key on Microsoft Computer keyboard with its logo displayed on it. Search for this ⊞ on your keyboard.

Apple Key: This also known as Command key is a modifier key that you can find on an Apple keyboard. It usually has the image of an apple or command logo on it. Search for this on your Apple keyboard ⌘

Function Keys: These are keys that have **F** on them which are usually combined with other keys. They are F1 - F12, and are also in the class called *Special Keys*.

Special Keys: These are keys that perform special functions. They include: Tab, Ctrl, Caps lock, Insert, Prt sc, alt gr, Shift, Home, Num lock, Esc, and many others. Special keys differ according to the type of computer involved. In some keyboard layout, especially laptops, the keys that turn the speaker on/off, the one that increases/decreases volume, the key that turns the computer Wifi on/off are also special keys.

Other Special Keys Worthy of Note:

Enter Key: This is located at the right-hand corner of most keyboards. It is used to send messages to the computer to execute commands, in most cases it is used to mean "Ok" or "Go".

Escape Key (ESC): This is the first key on the upper left of most keyboards. It is used to cancel routines, close menus, and select options such as *Save* according to circumstance.

Control Key (CTRL): It is located on the bottom row of the left and right hand side of the keyboard. They also work with the function keys to execute commands using Keyboard shortcuts (key combinations).

Alternate Key (ALT): It is located on the bottom row also of some keyboard, very close to the CTRL key on both side of the keyboard. It enables many editing functions to be accomplished by using some keystroke combinations on the keyboard.

Shift Key: This adds to the roles of function keys. In addition, it enables the use of alternative function of a particular button (key), especially, those with more than one function on a key. E.g. use of capital letters, symbols, and numbers.

1.3. Selecting/Highlighting With Keyboard.

This is a highlighting method or style where data is selected using the computer keyboard instead of a computer mouse.

To do this:

- Move your cursor to the text or object you want to highlight, make sure that area is active,
- Hold down the shift key with one finger,
- Then use another finger to move the arrow key that points to the direction you want to highlight.

1.4 The Operating Modes Of The Keyboard.

Just like the computer mouse, keyboard has two operating modes. The two modes are Text Entering Mode and Command Mode.

a. **Text Entering Mode:** this mode gives the operator/user the opportunity to type text.

b.　**Command Mode:** this is used to command the operating system/software/application to execute commands in certain ways.

2. Ways To Improve In Your Typing Skill.

1. Put Your Eyes Off The Keyboard.

This is the aspect of keyboard usage that many don't find funny because they always ask. "How can I put my eyes off the keyboard when I am running away from the occurrence of errors on my file?" My aim is to be fast, is this not going to slow me down?

Of course, there will be errors and at the same time your speed will slow down but the motive behind the introduction of this method is to make you faster than you are. Looking at your keyboard while you type can make you get a sore neck, it is better you learn to touch type because the more you type with your eyes fixed on the screen instead of the keyboard, the faster you become.
An alternative to keeping your eyes off your keyboard is to use the *"Das Keyboard Ultimate"*.

2. Errors Challenge You
It is better to fail than to not try at all. Not trying at all is an attribute of the weak and lazybones. When you

make mistakes, try again because errors are opportunities for improvement.

3. Good Posture (Position Yourself Well).
Do not adopt an awkward position while typing. You should get everything on your desk organized or arranged before sitting to type. Your posture while typing contributes to your speed and productivity.

4. Practice
Here is the conclusion of everything said above. You have to practice your shortcuts constantly. The practice alone is a way of improvement. "Practice brings improvement". Practice always.

Software That Will Help You Improve on Your Typing Skill.

There are several Software programs for typing that both kids and adults can use for their typing skill. Here is a list of software that can help you improve on your typing: Mavis Beacon, Typing Instructor, Mucky Typing Adventure, Rapid Tying Tutor, Letter Chase Tying Tutor, Alice Touch Typing Tutor and many more. Look for the ones you love. Personally, I love Mavis Beacon.

To learn typing using MAVIS BEACON, install Mavis Beacon software on your computer, start with keyboard lesson, then move to games. Games like *Penguin Crossing, Creature Lab*, or *Space Junk* will help you become a professional in typing. Typing and keyboard shortcuts work hand-in-hand.

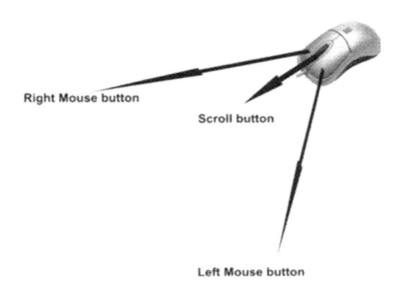

Right Mouse button

Scroll button

Left Mouse button

3. Mouse:

This is an oval-shaped portable input device with three buttons for scrolling, left clicking, and right clicking that enables work to be done effectively on a computer. The plural form of mouse is mice.

3.1 Types of Computer Mouse

- Mechanical Mouse.
- Optical Mechanical Mouse (Optomechanical).
- Laser Mouse.
- Optical Mouse.
- BlueTrack Mouse.

3.2 Forms of Clicking:

Left Clicking: This is the process of clicking the left side button of the mouse. It can also be called *clicking* without the addition of *left*.

Right Clicking: It is the process of clicking the right side button of a computer mouse.

Double Clicking: It is the process of clicking the left side button two times (twice) and immediately.

Triple Clicking: It is the process of clicking the left side button three times (thrice) and immediately.

Double clicking is used to select a word while triple clicking is used to select a sentence or paragraph.

Scroll Button: It is the little key attached to the mouse that looks like a tiny wheel. It takes you up and down a page when moved.

3.3 Mouse Pad: This is a small soft mat that is placed under the mouse to make it have a free movement.

3.4 Laptop Mouse Touchpad

This unlike the mouse we explained above is not external, rather it is inbuilt (comes with the laptop computer). With the presence of a laptop mouse touchpad, an external mouse is not needed to use a laptop, except in a case where it is malfunctioning or the operator prefers to use external one for some reasons.

The laptop mouse touchpad is usually positioned at the end of the keyboard section of a laptop computer. It is rectangular in shape with two buttons positioned below it. The two buttons/keys are used for left and right clicking just like the external mouse. Some laptops come with four mouse keys. Two placed above the mouse for left and right clicking and two other keys placed below it for the same function.

4. Definition Of Keyboard Shortcuts.

Keyboard shortcuts are defined as a series of keys, most times with combination that execute tasks which typically involve the use of mouse or other input devices.

5. Why You Should Use Shortcuts.

1. One may not be able to use a computer mouse easily because of disability or pain.

2. One may not be able to see the mouse pointer as a result of vision impairment, in such case what will the person do? The answer is SHORTCUT.

3. Research has made it known that Extensive mouse usage is related to Repetitive Syndrome Injury (RSI) greatly than the use of keyboard.

4. Keyboard shortcuts speed up productivity, making learning them a worthwhile effort.

5. When performing a job that requires precision, it is wise that you use the keyboard instead of mouse, for instance, if you are dealing with Text Editing, it is better you handle it using keyboard shortcuts than spending more time doing it with your computer mouse alone.

6. Studies calculate that using keyboard shortcuts allows working 10 times faster than working with

the mouse. The time you spend looking for the mouse and then getting the cursor to the position you want is lost! Reducing your work duration by 10 times gives you greater results.

5.1 Ways To Become A Lover Of Shortcuts.

1. Always have the urge to learn new shortcut keys associated with the programs you use.
2. Be happy whenever you learn a new shortcut.
3. Try as much as you can to apply the new shortcuts you learnt.
4. Always bear it in mind that learning new shortcuts is worth it.
5. Always remember that the use of keyboard shortcuts keeps people healthy while performing computer activities.

5.2 How To Learn New Shortcut Keys
1. Do a research on them: quick references (a cheat sheet comprehensively compiled like ours) can go a long way to help you improve.
2. Buy applications that show you keyboard shortcuts every time you execute an action with mouse.
3. Disconnect your mouse if you must learn this fast.
4. Read user manuals and help topics (Whether offline or online).

5.3 Your Reward For Knowing Shortcut Keys.

1. You will get faster unimaginably.
2. Your level of efficiency will increase.
3. You will find it easy to use.
4. Opportunities are high that you will become an expert in what you do.
5. You won't have to go for **Office button**, click **New,** click **Blank and Recent**, and click on **Create** just to insert a fresh/blank page. **Ctrl +N** takes care of that in a second.

A Funny Note: Keyboarding and Mousing are in a marital union with Keyboarding being the head, so it will be unfair for anybody to put asunder between them.

5.4 Why We Emphasize On The Use of Shortcuts.

You may never leave your mouse completely unless you are ready to make your brain a box of keyboard shortcuts which will really be frustrating, just imagine yourself learning all shortcuts that go with the programs you use and their various versions. You shouldn't learn keyboard shortcuts that way.

Why we are emphasizing on the use of shortcuts is because mouse usage is becoming unusually common and unhealthy, too. So we just want to make sure both are combined so you can get fast, productive and healthy in your computer activities. All you need to know is just the most important ones associated with the programs you use.

CHAPTER 3

Keyboard Shortcuts in GIMP 2.8

Definition of Program: GIMP (GNU Image Manipulation Program) is a powerful open source graphics and digital imaging tool.

The following list contains keyboard shortcuts that will boost your productivity in GIMP 2.8.

File Menu Shortcuts

SHORTCUT	RESULT
Ctrl+N	New image
Shift+Ctrl+V	Create a new image from clipboard
Ctrl+1	Open recent image #1
Ctrl+2	Open recent image #2
Ctrl+3	Open recent image #3
Ctrl+4	Open recent image #4
Ctrl+5	Open recent image #5
Ctrl+6	Open recent image #6
Ctrl+7	Open recent image #7

Ctrl+8	Open recent image #8
Ctrl+9	Open recent image #9
Ctrl+0	Open recent image #10
Ctrl+O	Open image
Ctrl+Alt+O	Open as layers
Ctrl+S	Save image
Shift+Ctrl+S	Save As
Ctrl+P	Print
Ctrl+W	Close
Shift+Ctrl+W	Close all
Ctrl+Q	Quit

Tools Menu Shortcuts

General Shortcuts for tools

SHORTCUT	RESULT
B	Paths
D	Default Colors (click on the colours to change them)
O	Colour picker
T	Text
X	Swap Colours
Z	Zoom
Shift+M	Measure
Ctrl+B	Toolbox
Ctrl+F	Repeat last

Shift+Ctrl+F	Re-show Last

Shortcuts for selection tools

SHORTCUT	RESULT
Shift+O	Select by colour
E	Ellipse Select
F	Free Select
I	Intelligent Scissors
R	Rectangle select
U	Fussy Select

Shortcuts for transform tools

SHORTCUT	RESULT
M	Move
Q	Align
Shift+C	Crop
Shift+F	Flip
Shift+P	Perspective
Shift+R	Rotate
Shift+S	Shear
Shift+T	Scale

Shortcuts for Paint tools

SHORTCUT	RESULT
Shift+B	Bucket Fill
Shift+D	Dodge / Burn

Shift+E	Eraser
Shift+U	Sharpen /Blur
A	Airbrush
C	Clone
K	Ink
L	Blend
N	Pencil
p	Paintbrush
S	Smudge

Edit Menu Shortcuts

SHORTCUT	RESULT
Ctrl+Z	Undo
Ctrl+Y	Redo
Ctrl+C	Copy
Ctrl+X	Cut
Ctrl+V	Paste
Delete	Clear
Shift+Ctrl+C	Copy Visible
Shift+Ctrl+V	Paste as new image
Ctrl+,	Fill with FG Color
Ctrl+.	Fill with BG Color
Ctrl+;	Fill with Pattern

Windows Menu Shortcuts

Dockable Dialogs

SHORTCUT	RESULT
Ctrl+B	Toolbox
Ctrl+G	Gradients
Ctrl+L	Layers
Shift+Ctrl+B	Brushes
Shift+Ctrl+P	Patterns

View Menu Shortcuts

SHORTCUT	RESULT
Ctrl+E	Shrink Wrap (Reduce image window to size of image)
Ctrl+C	Show Selection
F11	Toggle Full Screen view
Shift+Ctrl+R	Show Rulers
Shift+Ctrl+T	Show Guides

Layer Menu Shortcuts

SHORTCUT	RESULT
Shift+Ctrl+N	New Layer
Shift+Ctrl+D	Duplicate Layer

Ctrl+H	Anchor layer
Page Up	Select Previous Layer
Page Down	Select Next Layer
Home	Select Top Layer
End	Select Bottom Layer

Select Menu Shortcuts

SHORTCUT	RESULT
Ctrl+A	Select All
Ctrl+I	Invert Selection
Shift+Ctrl+A	Select None
Shift+Ctrl+L	Create a floating selection
Shift+O	Select by colour
Shift+V	Select from Path
Shift+Q	Toggle Quick Mask

Image Menu Shortcuts

SHORTCUT	RESULT
Ctrl+D	Duplicate image
Ctrl+M	Merge visible layers
Alt+Return	Display image properties

Zoom Tool Shortcuts

SHORTCUT	RESULT
Click	Zoom in
Ctrl+Click	Zoom out
Mouse drag	Zoom into the area

Help Menu Shortcuts

SHORTCUT	RESULT
F1	Help
Shift+F1	Context Sensitive Help

Creating Shortcuts to Menu Functions

Many functions which are accessible via the image menu have a default keyboard shortcut. You may want to create a new shortcut for a command that you use a lot and doesn't have one or, more rarely, edit an existing shortcut. There are two methods for doing this.

Procedure Using Dynamic Keyboard Shortcuts

1. First, you have to activate this capability by checking the Use dynamic keyboard shortcuts option in the Interface item of the *Preferences* menu. This option is usually not checked, to prevent accidental key presses from creating an unwanted shortcut.

2. While you're doing that, also check the Save keyboard shortcuts on exit option so that your shortcut will be saved.

3. To create a keyboard shortcut, simply place the mouse pointer on a command in the menu: it will then be highlighted. Be careful that the mouse pointer doesn't move and type a sequence of three keys, keeping the keys pressed. You will see this sequence appear on the right of the command.

4. It is best to use the **Ctrl** + **Alt** + **Key** sequence for your custom shortcuts.

Configure Keyboard Shortcuts

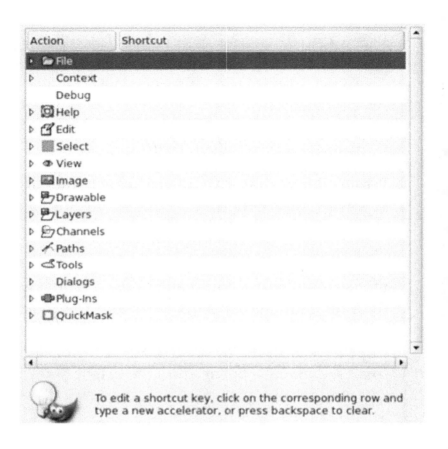

To edit a shortcut key, click on the corresponding row and type a new accelerator, or press backspace to clear.

Procedure 12.2. Using the Keyboard Shortcut Editor

1. You get to this Editor by clicking on **Configure keyboard shortcuts** in the "Interface" item of the *Preferences* menu.

2. As shown in this dialog, you can select the command you want to create a shortcut for, in the "Action" area. Then you type your key sequence as above. In principle, the Space bar should clear a shortcut. (In practice, it clears it, but doesn't delete it.)

3. This shortcut editor also allows you to *control the tool parameter settings* with the keyboard. At the top of this dialog, you can find a Context menu that takes you to the tool parameters. To make your work easier, tool types are marked with small icons.

Note

Custom Keyboard shortcuts are stored in one of Gimp's hidden directory (/home/[username]/.gimp-2.8/menurc) under Linux. Under Windows, path varies according to version:

- C:\Documents and Settings\[Username]\.gimp-2.8\menurcunder Windows XP.

- C:\Program Files\GIMP 2\etc\gimp\2.0\menurc under Windows 7.

- C:\Programmes\GIMP
  2\etc\gimp\2.0\menurc under Windows 10.

More, this location may change if GIMP is
installed after having already installed Git
Bash or Cygwin. In this case, they will
appear in C:\Program Files\Git\.gimp-
[version]\menurc.

**"menu.rc" is a simple text file that you can
transport from one computer to another.**

HOW TO GET YOUR COPY OF OUR 939-PAGE FULL COLOR GIMP BOOK.

First, we thank you for choosing GIMP 2.8 because if you didn't there won't be any need for a book like this.

Send an email to *contactucabelbooks@gmail.com* **for a copy of the 939-page full color GIMP book.**

We will be happy if you review this book.

Thank you.

Download Our EBooks Today For Free.

In order to appreciate our customers, we have made some of our titles available at 0.00. They are totally free. Feel free to get a copy of the free titles.

Here are books we give to our customers free of charge:

(1) For Keyboard Shortcuts in Windows check:

Windows 7 Keyboard Shortcuts.

(2) For Keyboard Shortcuts in Office 2016 for Windows check:

Word 2016 Keyboard Shortcuts For Windows.

(3) For Keyboard Shortcuts in Office 2016 for Mac check:

OneNote 2016 Keyboard Shortcuts For Macintosh.

Follow this link to download any of the titles listed above for free.

Note: Feel free to download them from our website or your favorite bookstore today. Thank you.

Other Books By This Publisher.

<u>Note:</u> Titles for single programs under Shortcut Matters series are not part of this list.

S/N	Title	Series
Series A: Limits Breaking Quotes.		
1	Discover Your Key Christian Quotes	Limits Breaking Quotes
Series B: Shortcut Matters.		
1	Windows 7 Shortcuts	Shortcut Matters
2	Windows 7 Shortcuts & Tips	Shortcut Matters
3	Windows 8.1 Shortcuts	Shortcut Matters
4	Windows 10 Shortcut Keys	Shortcut Matters
5	Microsoft Office 2007 Keyboard Shortcuts For Windows.	Shortcut Matters
6	Microsoft Office 2010 Shortcuts For Windows.	Shortcut Matters
7	Microsoft Office 2013 Shortcuts For Windows.	Shortcut Matters
8	Microsoft Office 2016 Shortcuts For Windows.	Shortcut Matters
9	Microsoft Office 2016 Keyboard Shortcuts For Macintosh.	Shortcut Matters
10	Top 11 Adobe Programs Keyboard Shortcuts	Shortcut Matters
11	Top 10 Email Service Providers Keyboard Shortcuts	Shortcut Matters
12	Hot Corel Programs Keyboard Shortcuts	Shortcut Matters

13	Top 10 Browsers Keyboard Shortcuts	Shortcut Matters
14	Microsoft Browsers Keyboard Shortcuts.	Shortcut Matters
15	Popular Email Service Providers Keyboard Shortcuts	Shortcut Matters
16	Professional Video Editing with Keyboard Shortcuts.	Shortcut Matters
17	Popular Web Browsers Keyboard Shortcuts.	Shortcut Matters

Series C: Teach Yourself.

1	Teach Yourself Computer Fundamentals	Teach Yourself
2	Teach Yourself Computer Fundamentals Workbook	Teach Yourself

Series D: For Painless Publishing

1	Self-Publish it with CreateSpace.	For Painless Publishing
2	Where is my money? Now solved for Kindle and CreateSpace	For Painless Publishing
3	Describe it on Amazon	For Painless Publishing